FIGHTER PLANES

A Postcard Book™

RUNNING PRESS
PHILADELPHIA, PENNSYLVANIA

Canadian representatives: General Publishing Co., Ltd., 30 Lesmill Road, Don Mills, Ontario M3B 2T6.
International representatives: Worldwide Media Services, Inc., 115 East Twenty-third Street, New York, New York 10010.

9   8   7   6   5   4   3   2   1
The digit on the right indicates the number of this printing.

ISBN 0-89471-822-3

Research consultant: Robert R. Ropelewski
Cover design by Toby Schmidt
Interior Design by Eric Walker
Front cover photograph copyright © Jeff Ethell/International Defense Images (IDI)
Back cover photograph copyright © Joe Cupido/IDI
Title page photograph copyright © Joe Cupido/IDI

Typography by Commcor Communications Corporation, Philadelphia, Pennsylvania.
Printed and bound in the United States of America by Innovation Printing.
This book may be ordered by mail from the publisher. Please add $2.50
for postage and handling. *But try your bookstore first!*
Running Press Book Publishers, 125 South Twenty-second Street, Philadelphia, Pennsylvania 19103

Of all the secrets of nature unlocked over the centuries, few have been as inspiring or as exhilarating as the magic of flight. None of the applications of flight has stimulated imaginations or stirred a sense of adventure and gallantry more than the fighter aircraft. Powerful and protective, yet savage and menacing, the fighter can trace a graceful arc across the sky or pitch and roll violently to take aim at a target or to avoid becoming one.

As visionary as they were, Wilbur and Orville Wright could not have foreseen the spectacular evolution of the airplane in the decades following the first flight of the Wright Flyer at Kitty Hawk, North Carolina, in 1903. Most of the significant advances in aviation in those subsequent decades were the direct result of the needs of fighter pilots.

"You can never give a fighter pilot enough speed, or enough range, or enough power," aircraft designers acknowledge, sometimes in exasperation. Used primarily for battlefield reconnaissance in the opening days of World War I, the earliest military aircraft could hardly carry a machine gun and ammunition without severely handicapping their performance. Rapid maneuvering was often difficult for planes not designed for such capabilities. But as pilots began taking aim at one another, and at enemy forces on the ground, airplane designers began modifying their aircraft. Each new generation of fighters brought with it significant improvements in engines, aerodynamics, and weaponry.

The advent of the jet engine in the closing days of World War II spelled a major revolution in fighter performance. By the time of the Korean War in the early 1950s, it was clear that the days of the propeller-driven fighter plane were past. While the fastest propeller-driven planes operated in the 300–400 mph range, the new jets flew closer to 600 mph and at altitudes 10–20,000 feet higher than the prop-driven fighters.

Electronic developments in the late 1950s spawned another revolution. Airborne radar became practical, allowing pilots to spot an approaching enemy aircraft well beyond the range of the naked eye, and missiles extended the striking range of the fighters.

A new generation of fighters appeared in the early 1970s, consolidating engine technology, aerodynamic innovations, and computer-driven flight controls. The ability to fly at speeds above Mach 2—twice the speed of sound—became commonplace, though seldom used. Fighter radar detection ranges and the striking distance of new air-to-air missiles reached beyond 100 miles, and the expanded power of modern jet engines permitted new attack fighters to carry heavier weapon loads than many of the largest bombers of World War II. Higher altitudes also could be reached, although the effective use of surface-to-air missile systems at higher altitudes has kept most fighters from using those altitudes in combat. Ground-mapping radar, advanced navigation systems, and night vision devices have given fighter-attack pilots the option of penetrating enemy airspace at altitudes of only a few hundred feet, day or night, using high terrain to mask their planes from enemy radar and missiles until they reach their targets.

Even in peacetime, fighter planes continue to evolve. Every year new capabilities are added to existing fighters, and on the drawing board an entirely new generation of aircraft—faster, higher-flying, and harder to detect with today's radar—is now taking shape.

With its spreading variable-sweep wings, the F-111 is capable of flying faster than the speed of sound at sea level—a feat that many fighters cannot accomplish. © Erik Simonsen/IDI

FIGHTER PLANES POSTCARD BOOK™   *RUNNING PRESS BOOK PUBLISHERS*

The F-14 is one of the largest planes. Despite its size, it handles well in dogfights. © Kirby Harrison/IDI

FIGHTER PLANES POSTCARD BOOK™   *RUNNING PRESS BOOK PUBLISHERS*

Fighter planes use a catapult to take off from the decks of aircraft carriers. During the launching phase, planes leave the deck of the carrier every 35 to 45 seconds.
© Frederick Sutter/IDI

FIGHTER PLANES POSTCARD BOOK™   *RUNNING PRESS BOOK PUBLISHERS*

The F-14 Tomcat was popularized in the movie "Top Gun." Trainees at the U.S. Navy Top Gun School fly Tomcats in mock air battles with instructors. © Joe Cupido/IDI

FIGHTER PLANES POSTCARD BOOK™   *RUNNING PRESS BOOK PUBLISHERS*

Flown by the U.S. Marine Corps, the AV–8B can hover in the air and land vertically by directing the thrust of its engines. © Frank Mormillo/IDI

FIGHTER PLANES POSTCARD BOOK™   *RUNNING PRESS BOOK PUBLISHERS*

The F-4 Phantom is armed with a variety of missiles. When enemy radar locks onto this plane, the Phantom crew fires missiles that retrace the radar signals to their source. © Mi Seitelman/IDI

FIGHTER PLANES POSTCARD BOOK™   *RUNNING PRESS BOOK PUBLISHERS*

The pilot sits in the front and a weapons systems officer or radar operator sits in the rear of the F-4 Phantom. © Frederick Sutter/IDI

FIGHTER PLANES POSTCARD BOOK™   *RUNNING PRESS BOOK PUBLISHERS*

Once a powerful flying force, the F-4 is slowly disappearing as new, faster, more maneuverable jets enter service. © Frederick Sutter/IDI

FIGHTER PLANES POSTCARD BOOK™   *RUNNING PRESS BOOK PUBLISHERS*

The size and performance of the F-5 closely resemble those of many enemy aircraft. For this reason, the F-5 is widely used in fighter training to simulate enemy planes.
© Mi Seitelman/IDI

FIGHTER PLANES POSTCARD BOOK ™   *RUNNING PRESS BOOK PUBLISHERS*

The F-5 was originally constructed for sale to foreign countries with developing air forces. © Mi Seitelman/IDI

FIGHTER PLANES POSTCARD BOOK™   *RUNNING PRESS BOOK PUBLISHERS*

Used primarily as a defense aircraft, the F–106 has never been in actual combat. These planes are gradually being taken out of service by the U.S. Air Force and the U.S. Air National Guard. © Jeff Ethell/IDI

FIGHTER PLANES POSTCARD BOOK™   *RUNNING PRESS BOOK PUBLISHERS*

The A-4 "Skyhawk" (bottom) is flown by instructors at the U.S. Navy's Top Gun School, where its superior dogfight performance against more conventional fighters has earned it the nickname "Mongoose." © Mi Seitelman/IDI

FIGHTER PLANES POSTCARD BOOK™   *RUNNING PRESS BOOK PUBLISHERS*

An SR-71 prepares to refuel. A probe is lowered from a tanker plane that connects with an intake on the top of the SR-71. © Jeff Ethell/IDI

FIGHTER PLANES POSTCARD BOOK™   *RUNNING PRESS BOOK PUBLISHERS*

Primarily a reconnaissance plane, the SR–71 flies on fact-gathering missions high in the earth's troposphere. It collects technical information unavailable to space satellites. © Erik Simonsen/IDI

Nicknamed the "aardvark," this fighter-bomber can perform high-speed, low-altitude bombing missions day or night in any weather. © Joe Cupido/IDI

FIGHTER PLANES POSTCARD BOOK™   *RUNNING PRESS BOOK PUBLISHERS*

The spreading, variable-sweep wings of the F–14 make it aerodynamically efficient in high-speed combat and in landing at low speeds. © Frederick Sutter/IDI

FIGHTER PLANES POSTCARD BOOK™   *RUNNING PRESS BOOK PUBLISHERS*

Excellent in long range and close-combat situations, the F–15 "Eagle" has been proven a successful fighter against Soviet MiGs © Mi Seitelman/IDI

FIGHTER PLANES POSTCARD BOOK™   *RUNNING PRESS BOOK PUBLISHERS*

The versatile, single-pilot F-15 has been deployed in both Europe and the Mideast, where it is relied upon to take immediate action in emergencies. © Mi Seitelman/IDI

FIGHTER PLANES POSTCARD BOOK™   *RUNNING PRESS BOOK PUBLISHERS*

The F-15 is not deployed on aircraft carriers. These planes were designed for overland use by the U.S. Air Force and the U.S. Air National Guard. © Frank Mormillo/IDI

FIGHTER PLANES POSTCARD BOOK™   *RUNNING PRESS BOOK PUBLISHERS*

Known as the ''Hornet,'' the
F/A-18 is both a fighter and a
bomber. © Mi Seitelman/IDI

The Hornet has a transparent control display positioned in the pilot's line of vision. This feature enables the pilot to monitor important plane functions while engaged in combat. © Frank Mormillo/IDI

FIGHTER PLANES POSTCARD BOOK™   *RUNNING PRESS BOOK PUBLISHERS*

The Hornet can be launched from aircraft carriers and from land bases. Catapult officers maintain contact with the pilot and the air boss in the control tower. © Kirby Harrison/IDI

FIGHTER PLANES POSTCARD BOOK™   *RUNNING PRESS BOOK PUBLISHERS*

Chiefly a bomber, the A–7 Corsair II has eight separate weapons stations. © Mi Seitelman/IDI

FIGHTER PLANES POSTCARD BOOK™   *RUNNING PRESS BOOK PUBLISHERS*

The large air intake of the A-7 often sucks in objects that can damage the blades of its turbine engines. © Mi Seitelman/IDI

The F–16 Fighting Falcon (top) was a winner of NATO's fighter design competition. This fully computerized ''electric jet'' delivers superhuman G-forces that test the endurance of many pilots. © Joe Cupido/IDI

FIGHTER PLANES POSTCARD BOOK™   *RUNNING PRESS BOOK PUBLISHERS*

Frequently flown in formation, the
F–16 is the plane of choice for the
U.S. Air Force Flight Demonstration
Team known as the "Thunder-
birds." © Mi Seitelman/IDI

FIGHTER PLANES POSTCARD BOOK™   *RUNNING PRESS BOOK PUBLISHERS*

The A–10 Thunderbolt II, affectionately called the "Warthog" by its pilots, is a slow-moving, heavily armored weapons platform. It is designed to withstand ground fire while it flies low over enemy targets. © Mi Seitelman/IDI

Neither a fighter nor a bomber, the EA–6B "Prowler" carries powerful transmitters and other electronic equipment to jam enemy ground radar. Each plane carries one pilot and three electronic warfare experts. © Mi Seitelman/IDI

FIGHTER PLANES POSTCARD BOOK™   *RUNNING PRESS BOOK PUBLISHERS*

The first training jet used by the U.S. Air Force was the T–33 "T-Bird." These aircraft now serve as practice targets for fighter missile training.
© Jeff Ethell/IDI

FIGHTER PLANES POSTCARD BOOK™   *RUNNING PRESS BOOK PUBLISHERS*

The SR–71 is not a fighter plane, but it flies three times the speed of sound. Its specially constructed surface absorbs radar signals, making it difficult for ground-based search radar to detect. © Erik Simonsen/IDI

FIGHTER PLANES POSTCARD BOOK™   *RUNNING PRESS BOOK PUBLISHERS*